How to Keep Going when You Lose Someone You Love

A guide to coping with bereavement

and the grieving process

By

Benjamin Kennet

How to Keep Going when You Lose Someone You Love

Copyright © 2017

ISBN: 9781520260327

Warning and Disclaimer

Publisher Contact

Skinny Bottle Publishing

books@skinnybottle.com

Introduction

Learning how to keep going on after you have lost someone you love seems like an absolute impossibility at first. Everyone seems to have their own advice that they throw at you, and you know it's for good reason but it still doesn't even scrape the surface of the depth of pain that you feel. The good thing is that you really can get through the grieving process once you throw out a few of the most common myths that surround it.

The first thing you should realize is that the grieving process is unique to each individual. There isn't any one way that defines exactly how you should go about grieving. If you feel like crying every day until you are through it, then cry every day. If you don't feel emotional and in fact feel numb, understand that, too, is an important part of the grieving process.

Losing someone that is close to you will leave you feeling a wide range of emotions and some of them may make you feel like you are being completely childish. That is completely okay. As time goes by though you will learn how to examine these emotions and deal with them accordingly.

Remember that the grieving process takes time for everybody. Anybody that seems like they can bounce right back to life is only setting themselves up for a wave of emotions to come crashing down further on down the road in their life. The best thing that you can do is to allow yourself the time and brutal honesty it takes to face your hurt and fears head on.

There will be phases when you will go through cycles of the same feelings. Just when you think that you have finally accepted that your loved one is gone, you may find yourself overwhelmed with the undeniable feeling that you will never be able to get through it on your own. This is a natural course for the grieving process. Over time, if you face each of these moments with brevity, these recurrences will lessen.

Eventually, you will be able to approach your life with a new sense of joy. It's a different sense of joy than what you were used to. There is no denying that you have lost a loved one. But the memory of that person will soon become a fond memory that you can rely on to bring you hope, guidance, and even a deeper appreciation of the moments that you have in your own life.

A lot of people don't like talking about the grieving process. It's as if it is something that we don't really go through like people just mourn for a couple weeks and then go right back to living 'ordinary' life. The simple fact is that life will never be the same when you lose a loved one. Yes, it's true, there are certainly aspects of everyday life that can't be denied. You still have to work, raise children and attend to your daily maintenance. But the grieving process itself will continue over a course of time that could take months to even a year or two.

So long as you are approaching it in a healthy manner and you know that you are accepting of the fact that you have lost a loved one, you don't have to worry about how long it takes for you. When we lose someone we love we don't forget who they were. We carry the memory of them alive inside of us for life. As you reflect on your loved one there will always be moments when you are filled with sadness and longing. The important thing is that, with time, these moments won't be quite so intense and you will learn how to handle them.

Continuing your life after you have lost a loved one is a process of learning how to find your way in the world. You will build into a new person as you begin to explore people, places, and things that you may never have taken the time to do before. You will need to find things to fill the emotional space that your loved one once resided in. This doesn't mean that you necessarily are 'changing'.

It means that you are taking the time to realize that your life still has rich meaning in it. You will eventually go about exploring that meaning and it may take you down an adventure that you could never have imagined. Remember, though, this doesn't mean that you are going to forget your loved one.

Leading a new life, the one that is yours, is a way that you can honor your loved one by not allowing yourself to simply wallow in pain and suffering. The process isn't an easy one by any measure. When you need to, and you are ready to, don't be afraid to turn to those in your life that you trust for guidance. Look to friends and family to help support and guide you whenever you need them. Don't be afraid to even look into different organizations that offer support to people that are grieving.

It is your responsibility to own your emotions just as much as it is your responsibility to take care of yourself. Nobody else can do that job for you. While the following information that we cover can help you, please know that these are simply suggestions to help you moving on in your life. There is no set way. There are no rules, no guidelines. Only suggestions that you can take or leave on your own merit as you go through the process of grieving. Keep that in mind and you will make it through.

Getting to Know Grief

Grief comes in all sorts of shapes and sizes. When you are in the process of mourning the loss of a loved one you can expect to experience a wide arc of thoughts, feelings, and even physical responses. There is a strong tendency for many of us to feel at loss when trying to handle these experiences. What you must remember, is that everyone goes through them and that no matter how you are personally handling your grief, it is your grief. It isn't anybody else's.

Don't let another person dictate to you how you should be handling your feelings and thoughts. You may go through periods where you just don't want to talk to anybody and that is okay. At other time, you may feel like the room is spinning and you just can't get a grip on reality. These are all natural responses to grieving. Let's look at some more details about grief and the process of getting on with life after a deep loss.

All Types

First of all, grief can come from all sorts of different places. It doesn't have to necessarily be a person that you lost in order to feel grief. It can, in fact, be from the loss of not getting the promotion you were heavily relying on, or perhaps from becoming disabled and no longer able to use your body the way once did. It can come from realizing that perhaps your days of bearing children are no longer an option.

There is no greater loss than the death of a loved one. We all feel and experience things on our own level. Some people may handle the loss of a loved one really well, but the fact that they have thrown away their personal dreams is a grief they struggle with daily. Is one person's grief more extreme than another's? The answer is no. Grief is grief. It's never fun. But with the right approach, you can move the process along quicker than simply bottling it up.

This doesn't mean that you have to suddenly breakdown and have what some may think is the stereotypical reaction to handling loss. But it does mean that if you face your grief head on, immerse yourself in it, and then work proactively at handling it, you are more likely to overcome it quicker.

Here are some of the feelings that you will most likely encounter at one point or another along the path of grieving:

- Raging Anger

- Overwhelming Guilt

- Loss of Focus

- Deep Sorrow

- Depression

- Yearning or Longing

- Questioning of Faith

- Fear

No Time Line

The wild thing about grief is that even though you can go through the process and feel that you have healed completely, grief can still come around and revisit through life. The sorrow and separation that we experience when we lose something near to us forms a strong memory in our psyche. You may one day hear a song or smell something that reminds you of your loved one. This will trigger a reaction and make your heart sink a little bit. Understand these waves of emotion will get easier as time goes by and with each new wave that crashes into you, you won't be so overwhelmed. You will simply experience it without being completely carried away by it.

The process many go through on the time frame of their healing is usually a process of denial, argumentation, and then eventually acceptance. During the denial phase, you can expect that you just won't feel like what happened is even real. Days can go by and it will seem like you will never be able to adjust to your loss. Denial is an important part of the healing process because it actually slows things down for you a bit. It gives you time to process and digest what has actually happened at your own rate. Losing someone you love is one of the hardest things we go through in life. Our denial is simply a process of our mind taking the time to let our hearts accept what has happened.

The next phase is a phase of absolute confrontational behavior. It's also the angry phase, the time of extreme emotions, and the time of highest sensitivity. The illusion of denial has slowly begun to lift and what remains is the truth that things will never be the same. It's okay to act a little 'crazy' during this phase. In fact, you might feel like you are a little crazy but rest assured you are not. The intense feelings, or even complete lack of feeling, is a normal process. This is when those feelings mentioned earlier will be at the most advanced stage. You may even slip back into denial from time to time while you are going through this phase. Again, it is simply your mind's way of making sure that you digest everything accordingly.

What follows is a period of acceptance, that just like the denial phase, will come and go until it has officially settled in. You may even experience a bit of guilt as you enter into this phase. It's hard for all of us to start to feel like it is okay to let go of somebody. We don't want to dishonor our loved ones by simply moving on. It's as if pain must be continual in the absence of the deceased. Like we must always be mourning or else we could forget them. That if we move on, we are somehow devaluing our relationship with the departed. These feelings of guilt, also, will subside.

Loss is Loss

When we lose someone we might start noticing some left over feelings we may have experienced through the death of a different person that begin to resurface all over again. Many things influence your own particular situation and experience in grieving that you can never actually predict how it is going to hit you. One thing is for certain, the relationship that you had with the person will directly influence your psychology and what this loss means to you.

Different relationships will change the level of grieving. Somebody that never got a chance to tell someone they love them may grieve deeper than a three-month wife. Somebody that you don't get to actually say goodbye to is more than likely to leave a deep cut in your emotional state. If you believe the person that has passed away had led a good and rich life, then you may be more apt to actually focus on that, and not think about all the things they didn't get to do.

How You View Death

For some death is simply the natural process of life. It isn't anything to get too worked up about. They can appreciate life, and when death comes, they simply accept it as the way things go. Sure they grieve, but the grievance is accompanied with a scientific reasoning that changes the extent of their emotional hurt.

However, if you happen to have experienced a loss in your life that could have been prevented, your grieving is more likely to be prolonged due to feelings of guilt and responsibility. These will come in addition to all the other extreme emotions that we go through when somebody dies.

Even when it is clear that death could have been prevented, it is important to remember that there is no way of changing the past. If the death was unexpected and not due to prolonged illness, you are bound to feel like you have been hit blindsided and the grieving process will be more difficult.

Having a little notice that something is going to happen gives you a chance to prepare, not just emotionally, but also for all of the different necessary requisites like funerals, obituaries, and the aftermath. The longer the preparation period the more you will feel emotionally and physically drained. This will also make you feel more distant from what is happening. This isn't quite the same as the denial phase, and it is simply prolonging the grieving process for many. You will need to refuel yourself before you begin handling the scope of grieving.

Your Relationship with the Departed

It could be a spouse, a child, a parent, a distant family member, a sibling, a lover, a friend, even a completely distant but touching person in our lives. Each loss carries their own set of different emotions but in the end, loss is loss, no matter how you slice it. Depending on the relationship, were is what you should expect:

Your Spouse

The loneliness that ensues when you experience such a loss can be completely devastating as you attempt to reestablish balance without the person any longer in your life. If it was a spouse that you lost, you will find yourself needing to completely reexamine who you are. The person that once helped you define nearly every aspect of your life is no longer with you.

This period of rediscovery can take a while for some to step into. The frustration you feel is normal as you no longer have the same person by your side that filled many roles. Spouses don't just do compartmentalized roles in life. They fulfill and complete us. Often referred to as 'the better half', it's no wonder you will need to completely reinvent yourself to one degree or another.

Any and all financial dependency that you had may now be gone, and you may find the notion of having to tackle your own struggles 'on your own' even more difficult. This can lead to lethargy, depression, anger, and frustration. The important thing to focus on during widowhood is to develop new skills to handle the world that now confronts you. The significant loss you have experienced will leave you feeling like you will never again stand on your own two feet. But you will.

Your Parent

When we lose a parent as an adult, the loss can undeniably be one of the most complicated depending on the relationship that you had with your parent. There is a natural response to go back to a state of childhood. There is a strong sense that you shouldn't be feeling the 'outlandish' emotions that you feel.

The simple fact remains that they were your parent, and you were their child. There is no other relationship quite like this. The swinging feelings that experience may make you feel like you are not being responsible or an adult, but in fact, you are being responsible to the process of grieving and this is an important factor in healing.

Your Sibling

There is no set script that will be able to prepare you for all that will surface as you confront your loss and the meaning of it. When you lose a sibling you lose somebody that has been with you through everything in your childhood. That means that you lose somebody that can share with you all the times that you had, no matter what type of memories they were. It's like losing a part of a scrapbook almost. Without having somebody to share these memories with it can leave you with a feeling that the world is in disorder.

You, yourself, will examine your own mortality. It's also a frightening feeling to realize that your family is no longer the size that it was, and is, in fact, smaller. Recognizing the feelings of sadness and guilt that you may feel that others don't sympathize with you like you would expect. Some may not even know you had a sibling. It is almost like losing a child in the sense that you have lost a part of your own childhood. Despite a possible lack of adequate comforting from society during your grievance, you can still find people that do understand the loss you are experiencing.

Helping a Child Cope

When we help a child go through the process of grieving we are confronted with a completely different set of challenged that we must take into account. Depending on the child's age and emotional development they may not even be able to grasp what has happened and may think that the deceased is simply on vacation or is going to come back. The words that we use to convey what has happened can leave a lasting impact on the development and growth of that child's mental and emotional states well into adulthood. It is important to realize though that children are not immune to grieving. They absolutely do grieve. It is, therefore, important to be prepared and help them from becoming too overwhelmed while guiding them through the grieving process.

Limited Resources

Remember that a child doesn't have the same things at their disposal that you do. When they are frustrated and need to get away they should have adequate space to play. Remember what playing was for you as a child? It was a time of private thoughts and being able to think about things, sometimes without even actually having to 'think' about them. It's a way of processing. When a child wants to retire to playing, you should encourage them so that they can begin to work out the different feelings and thoughts that they are experiencing.

Children clearly lack the vocabulary that we have as adults. They don't understand the same things the same way. This is why you shouldn't say things like "Mommy went on a long vacation," or "Grandpa is up in the sky now". These sort of sayings don't help the child process grieving, and in fact, can make it even more difficult for them down the road when they are actually old enough to begin processing what has happened.

Anticipate Your Child's Needs

You also need to be very aware of what your child's needs will be. On top of your own grieving, remember that your child will be going through things on their own level. You can expect that they will be sad and completely overtaken by a whole slew of emotions that they have never experienced before. Let them know that you are there for them and that you are willing to talk about and answer any questions they may have.

In an ideal situation, you would have already begun preparing your child on the meaning of death, but that isn't always practical given the specific circumstances of your family's loss. It may seem like you want to cover up things for them by shrouding the death in religious beliefs or in euphemisms. The best course of action for you is to address the death directly. Let your child know the fact that it really is the end of life and that your loved one is truly gone.

The more direct you are and upfront, the better off your child will be able to realize what has happened. After the grieving process is well underway, if you feel the need to bring religious beliefs or philosophical beliefs to the table you can do so. But first, you must teach your child what death means on a very basic fundamental level.

Keep Your Child Present

You may feel that you don't want your child to be around at a funeral, or to participate in any of the activities surrounding the death of a loved one, but you are not protecting them. In fact, you are preparing them for more confusion and feelings of being alone as they are not allowed to be with all of the adults as part of the whole family. Remember having to sit at the small table at holiday times, where all the other children sat? Leaving your child out of the activities that adults undertake is even worse in terms of feelings of abandonment.

Instead, be proactive and make sure that the child can take part in these activities. Let them witness and see how adults grieve. Let them ask questions, and let them build the tools that they will need later on when they are old enough to begin digesting the totality of their loss.

It is important to remember that a child will experience their grief in phases throughout their life. This is because when they were younger they didn't have the ability to fully process and cope with what has happened. As these waves of realization occur you must do your best to support the child and not rely on them to take on different roles that the departed once fulfilled.

Resources for Tomorrow

After you have gone through the process of accepting that the death of your loved one has indeed happened, and you have completely immersed yourself in the complete agony and pain of it, you will come out the other side ready to start experiencing what it means to start living in the 'new' world without your loved one.

A Gradual Process

The grieving experience is slow and arduous, and so too is the period when you start to extend yourself out into the world again. You will not take off soaring like you are the happy-go-lucky person that you used to be. You can certainly get there again, but you will not do it overnight. Don't put excessive pressure on yourself to try and make it happen overnight either.

Allow yourself to start experiencing life again gradually. You will realize you are truly not alone, not by a long shot. As you do this you will keep confronting the fact that you have lost your loved one. Even though you have accepted it, you will keep reminding yourself of it. This is when you will learn how to truly adjust to the new life that you are living.

As these moments come up, you need to take the time to experience each one of them. There will be happy memories and the again the sad realization that your loved one is no longer near, and each of these will happen intermittingly. The intense feelings that you felt in the beginning of the grieving process won't be as intense this time around, but they are still the same feelings. You may feel that you are angry all over again, filled with deep remorse and guilt, and absolutely childish. These are passing emotions and they don't make you 'crazy' or out-of-control. They simply are part of getting back into the swing of living life without your loved one near you any longer.

Keeping Your Memory Alive

As time goes on you will find that you start to form a new kind of relationship with your deceased loved one. That person used to fill an actual physical space in your life, but now they have transformed into a mental relationship. You may feel it deep in your soul, that you are still connected to the person. Do not be afraid to keep them 'alive' in your memories.

This doesn't mean that you continue to go through life like they are still physically with you. You will need to redevelop your strength as an individual for an appropriate and healthy recovery. Keeping them 'alive' in your memory means that you allow yourself to be deeply touched and moved by the influence that the person had on your life. To forget the impact that they made would be a waste. You don't forget the love and joy that somebody shared with you when they are no longer with you.

You can turn to the memory of your loved one in times of need. Like when you are confronted with having to make a major life decision or even trying to remember how to make that famous casserole dish that everybody loved during the holiday season. These are the moments when you think about the ways that the departed handled life and you allow their guidance to influence the activities and decisions that you do today.

As you go through this process you will find that you want to focus on the good things that you shared with that person. Any bad memories are likely to hide in the shadows of the memory of the deceased. However, these memories are important to embrace as well. If you can construct a well-rounded view of them in your memory you can then choose the positive things that you want to remember. This also helps you confront the lessons that the person taught you when they were not that nice to you.

You will find that you can carry on conversations about your loved one, behave within their value system, and even embrace who you have become because of them by sharing some of their favorite sayings and actions. Volunteering in places where they did, doing things in their honor, and even simply thinking about all the wonderful memories that you had will help you keep them actively 'alive' in your life. These are also all healthy ways to keep developing your new identity without letting completely go of all the ways that your loved one touched your life.

A New You?

It is clear that there is now a new space in your life that has been created by the loss of your loved one. What you do with that space is up to you and is ultimately going to be one of the biggest deciding factors on how well will peacefully continue to fulfill your life. There is no set timeframe on when you should be starting to reenter the new world. Of course, after the grievance period searching for new relationships, new activities, and even sometimes new work, is better done sooner than later. This process is a way that you can start to take care of yourself by listening to your inner self.

It really isn't a 'new you'. You are still the same person as you once were when your loved one was present. But you no longer have that person around give them the attention, love and time you used to. Now that you have a space to fill, take the time to examine the different things that would make you feel happy to invest your time and emotions in. There may be things that you always wished of doing, or perhaps if you have no idea what to do then ask around. Different volunteer organizations can help you get out of your house and get more involved with the community. Just by getting yourself out and about, you will soon start to get in touch with yourself again.

If you have lost your spouse or husband, you don't need to jump into a relationship right away. Just take the time to nurture the 'new you', which is actually the only 'you' that there is. We invest a lot of emotional energy into our loved ones and when they pass we don't really know what to do with that energy. It may not feel at all like a luxury, but if you take the time to focus on yourself, you will find that you can embrace a life that is completely new to you while still keeping the memory of your loved one 'alive'.

Conclusion

With time, your grieving will pass and you will find that you can lead a fulfilling life without your loved one nearby. Keeping the memory of them alive is as simple as you want to make it. You can build a routine that you follow in the morning or evening, you can talk to people about them, you can carry yourself with the integrity and values that they instilled in you, or you can simply take small moments through the day to ponder on them.

The important thing to remember is that no two people grieve in the same way. Even though we have covered some important guidelines in how to move forward in your life after losing a loved one, they are simply that: guidelines. The easiest thing for you to do in the beginning is to remember that you are free to feel the full gambit of emotions. You can take your own time to do what you need to do to shelter the pain that you have experienced.

If other people try to tell you how to handle things, you can express your gratitude and move on about your day. Remember that others mean well and they simply want to let you know that they are there for you. Some people just don't express that very well.

When people do give you advice don't hesitate to take the opportunity to see if perhaps there is some truth in what they are saying. Often times if you try just a little you can find a kernel of wisdom in even the most cliché of statements. Things like, "It gets better." and "Stay strong." are certainly run-of-the-mill statements that you may hear from time to time. Take them for what they are.

The emotions that you are going to experience are going to be some of the most intense and extreme emotions you've ever felt in your life. As they come flowing through you, do your best to examine each one of them. The sooner you can face these emotions and see them for what they are the quicker you will find a way to express them, and you should express them.

Finding a healthy way for you to experience and vent your emotions might not be something that you are accustomed to. Everyone has a different approach that works for them. Some people like to get really physical and will go to the gym or go take it all out on the pillows until the feeling is out. Others use tools like painting or making music to bang out the intense waves of emotion that are sure to come when the loss of a loved one occurs.

If you can tap into your grieving process and make something productive of it, you have the chance to keep your life in balance along the way. As an adult, you don't get to turn off the real world. You still have bills to pay, you still have to work, and you may even have children to care for. Needless to say, you have responsibilities that can't be put on hold while you are grieving.

If you take a proactive approach to digging into the belly of your pain and examining all of it for what it is you can move through it fully. Leaving unfinished emotional business will simply put further strain on you. This can cause enough stress to make you feel like you are burning the candle at both ends. Getting back on your everyday life will seem a lot harder because you still have a weight of emotional baggage resting on your shoulders.

Realize that there is no hurry to get through grieving. Just do everything at your own rate. What is most important is that you do it, though. You will learn that many of the things that surface along the grieving process seem to have nothing to do with the loss you have experienced. There will be times when you are faced with practical problems, like handling an estate, or managing your own bills. Even something as simple as adjusting your grocery list will be part of the grieving process.

By working on yourself and giving yourself the emotional and physical attention that you need you will find that you can have the life that your loved one would want you to have.

Overcoming the loss of a loved one is not about forgetting them. It's about making sure that you are able to function fully and continue to live a rewarding life. You can do this while keeping the memory of them alive. It is possible.

If you need further help, do not hesitate to reach out to your friends, your family, and even different organizations if you need to. The most important things now involve you taking care of yourself and realizing that you are still here living. You need to live now. And yes, you can keep going and living after someone you still love has died.

Win a free

kindle
OASIS

Let us know what you thought of this book to enter the sweepstake at:

http://booksfor.review/keepgoing

Made in United States
North Haven, CT
13 August 2024

56037037R00017